Praise for *The language of bees*:

'This rich and assured debut, clearly the distillation of
well worth waiting for. A mature, finely crafted collect
most intimate details of her own life and on a wide kn
us how all are linked. As her epigram says, "We are nat___ ___ __ __ __ · ___ ___

'Howells' writing is assured and muscular, yet also as diaphanous and magical as a moth's wing,
fusing the enchantment of nature with the stark realities of living in our troubled world. She
reminds us of the cycles of life and death we are all tied to, and that we ignore at our peril.' –
The Western Mail

'...deeply haunting – a book you'll want to return to for multiple explorations, and which
will give more every time.' – *South Wales Evening Post*

'We are taken into a micro, alternate world, somewhat distant from the looming, threatening
backdrop of human activities that destroy [bees'] habitats and threaten global insect
populations. This microscopic focus, from a poet who harvests lavender from a Gower field,
enables us to gain an unexpected look back at human existence. The lyrical density of the
poems, their thick sound patterning and onomatopoeia, together with profuse, layered imagery,
make this book a rich visual and sonic experience.' – *Black Bough*

'Writing with a sense of bee-ness, her perspective couples acute attention to detail with concern
for species' survival. Howells draws on bees and their life cycle not only for vocabulary but
also as an extraordinary and rich source of metaphor to enable her to broach subject matter
both personal and painful. It's a delight to share her excitement at being in, and her care for,
the natural world' – *The Friday Poem*

'The themes of grief, death, loss, remembrance and love permeate Rae's poems. In her work,
there is not only the grief of losing a child expressed but also the grief of how the Earth is
being managed by humans. She is a skilled observer of the Natural World and of Human
Nature, too, and is not afraid to tackle difficult themes in her work, but does so with
sensitivity.' – *Pilgrim House*

'Howells' poetry is clever, surprising, transmuting the world into what it truly is: a constant
and consistent miracle. Some of these poems are prize-winning, and one can easily see why;
if "bees make music", so too does Howells in this book.' – *Buzz Magazine*

The language of bees is a collection bursting with the beauty and life of the natural world. In
these ambitious and accomplished poems, Rae Howells forges a unique and sparkling language,
which is capable of giving us all the wonder and richness, the multi-sensual onslaught, of the
world around us. Whether the subject is an interaction with a wasp or a mermaid, the thoughts
of trees or the feelings of a mother, the poems continually boom with so much life. The reader
is left with the poems' unforgettable phrases, their emotive impact and, more than anything
else, the excitement that happens when a voice so fully itself meets subject matter of the
greatest importance. On page after page, the power of these poems has us looking up, wanting
to shout *Hey world! Look at this!* ' – **Jonathan Edwards**

Rae Howells is a poet, journalist, academic and lavender farmer from Swansea. She's won both the Welsh International and Rialto Nature and Place poetry competitions. Her work has featured in a wide range of journals including *Magma, The Rialto, Poetry Wales, New Welsh Review, Acumen, Envoi, Poetry Ireland, Black Bough, Marble* and *The Cardiff Review*, as well as in the Poetry Business anthology, *The Result is What You See Today*, and the Arachne Press anthology, *A470*. Howells' pamphlet *Bloom and Bones*, co-authored with Jean James, was published by The Hedgehog Poetry Press in 2021. *The language of bees* is her first full collection.

raehowells.co.uk

The language of bees

Rae Howells

PARTHIAN

Parthian, Cardigan SA43 1ED
www.parthianbooks.com
First published in 2022
© Rae Howells 2022
ISBN 978-1-913640-69-9
Editor: Susie Wildsmith
Cover design by Emily Courdelle
Typeset by Elaine Sharples
Printed and bound by 4edge Limited, UK
Published with the financial support of the Welsh Books Council
British Library Cataloguing in Publication Data
A cataloguing record for this book is available from the British Library.

For Phil

I'll place royal jelly in your coffin
for your last flight
and close the moonlit petals of your face.

– Pascale Petit, 'The Bee Mother'

We are nature and it is us, and the extinction of the living world is our suicide. Not one sparrow can now be beneath notice, not one bee.

– Jay Griffiths, *Why Rebel*

CONTENTS

1   Honey
2   It took too long to learn the language of bees
4   *Dying bee in a takeaway box (1)* Once a bee
5   Whispers
6   A dead bee in the watering can
7   The Dunns
8   *Dying bee in a takeaway box (2)* Hydrangeas
9   You took me to the art house
10   Wind attempts a fox
12   *Dying bee in a takeaway box (3)* Autobiography
13   The honey jar
14   Rising through stars
15   River Aire
17   The Mermaid
20   Airlings
22   Ninety-eight earth days
23   *Dying bee in a takeaway box (4)* Out of time
24   Lambs
26   The world begins & ends a billion, billion times
28   there was a time they were knotted to the riverbank
30   Window
32   *Dying bee in a takeaway box (5)* Ironic syrup recipe (for bees)
33   Crowsong
34   *Dying bee in a takeaway box (6)* Medicine
35   The sacred well speaks to Mererid
37   The Llanlleonfel church yew
39   Wasps
40   *Dying bee in a takeaway box (7)* Wild colony collapse
41   *Dying bee in a takeaway box (8)* Clock
42   Woodthinking
44   *Dying bee in a takeaway box (9)* Body
45   Gaslight
47   You can play water
48   *Dying bee in a takeaway box (10)* Queen

49 Sonication

50 The swing

52 *Dying bee in a takeaway box (11)* Spark

53 In two hearts

59 The Green Pages

61 Silverfish live on my daughters' crumbs

62 *Dying bee in a takeaway box (12)* Wind

64 A dead bee in the Lego

65 The Circle

67 *Dying bee in a takeaway box (13)* Below the fold

68 Bread and butter

69 School run

70 The winter-king

71 Bee in a January Pilates Class

72 Silk buttons

74 Stories

Notes
Acknowledgments

Honey

I take off all my clothes
& stand before you
no longer the narrow-hipped queen of my youth
but a summer's end bee,
bumble-round, part-faded,
my furze worn bare. I have visited each flower
& visited again.
I know them all. Birdsfoot. Speedwell. Selfheal. Thrift.

What next? I ask,
my apple blossom breasts
wilting, and yet still, perhaps,
promising honey.
You, a seedhead, pulled
apart by the breeze, your hands
uncurling like a butterfly's tongue,
murmur:
what next?

It took too long to learn the language of bees

But in a field
sitting among dandelion, nettle, bramble, lavender,
I began to fathom it.

I had been agreeing
with the general sounds of the meadow:
the crunch of vegetation and
the clicks of small feet on soil and
the throats of birds flung open to let out blue –

meanwhile bees called by,
knocking into dock leaves,
humming and dusting themselves with pollen,
going about their seedpearl work

and I, kneeling, untethered weeds from around the crop
             as if lovingly unbuttoning the earth's shirt –

thought how two thousand years ago
Romans would have heard these same sounds
stood on this same warm rise,
smelled this ancient lavender on their skin,
heard these bees – or not *these* bees, but *bees* – and called '*apis!*'
how they would have dripped honey on hard bread
as they clipped coins to give change
             in the time of Emperor Constantine,
discarding their chipped vases for us to find.

And then at my shoulder
as if someone had read aloud a glossary,
I found I knew the words spoken by this hiveborn voice,
that here was more than a simple dash to join the dots between flowers,
             but Morse code, an SOS,
the bass clef come to life
a lisping alarm dragging through air that was – after all – much too hot.

I understood as they came
fussing about my head
like lost words,
their pollen baskets yellow and full,
wanting to seal this heat in wax for a long winter.

They worried about who might survive
this nicotined field to find my old secateurs,
scrape clean my dirty coins, discover
the shape my knees once pressed into furrows.

Dying bee in a takeaway box (1)
Once a bee

I was once a bee dying from my heart outwards
like paper in flames
alight
and then coaling myself to stillness
ossifying here in this somehow box
fabled half forgotten
only mothers knew my name.
I was fur on their bumbling tongues
there I lay a byline of myself
a slander of alive on a newspaper
while spring's green shuddered in my feet.
I was distant lightning
and every moment—   lightening
my body's weight slipping from me.
I lingered on its brim
balanced on a small wish that my wings might
refind their purpose
grasp themselves up into air.
but there was only this paper stillness.

Whispers

In France, before you loved me,
it was summer, and a strange blizzard fell.
Pale moths, each unique as a snowflake,
flurried in whispers from darkness
until the pavements grew
white beneath their paper bodies,
and cars slowed with their windscreen wipers flailing
against the ultrasonic ecstasy
of sky rubbing up against sky.

It was an ash squall,
a mating storm. Electric.
Everything sheathed beneath a skin of moths.

We sat at a small table on the bridge café
with side plates of sweet fig tart, coffee,
watching moths perform their final act of love and
fall from the sky's black mouth,
thickening the lamplight,
glancing down our naked shoulders to the street
before slipping into the black river.

And in the tumult I waited to see if you would kiss me.

The kiss came in its own shape:
a single moth swooned against my lips,
a fingertip's brush,
while you looked the other way,
over the water, thought of something else.
I found my mouth had been winged, stunned,
altered by the sky's dying touch.
It was the waiter who noticed, & opened the parasol
to stop the bodies falling
onto the crumbed moons of our plates.

A dead bee in the watering can

It became difficult to water the flowers
as if a blockage or a lack of tear ducts
might have gummed something up.

Sometimes the rose *would* get silted
with dandelion seeds or pollen or leaves
but even after rinsing the fitting

the water remained reluctant. I poured and tipped
and removed the rose again and then, finally,
with an umbilical gush the head

of a bee emerged from the spout. Not knowing
if something might still be done to save her
I gently tweezed and poured, until the small body

was delivered, her feet and wings neat as a newborn's.
I blew on her littleness – the packed-up legs, glimmering
wings. But she could not be distracted from

her heart's infinite hush.

The Dunns

After Edward Thomas

Yes, I remember the Dunns –
the pun of that pained twist of death
where all that could be done was done
despairingly. But was not enough.

Days we lay, curled like prawns in the arms
of a brown leather sofa, crying for
the death we knew would come
as sure as rain, but hoped would not.

It was a quick shove in the end,
a cut and push of muscles and slipped
mess, soft as a bag of black velvet
left out in the wet too long, and lost.

The curl of wax in the water was the only sign:
black folding back to black.
The clouds parted for us, then,
and we saw a crowd of shining stars, like tiny hands.

Dying bee in a takeaway box (2)
Hydrangeas

September on a train threading between
acid blue and pink gardens,
comes news of the catastrophic collapse
of world insect populations.

It is a distant piece of news,
a cousin's diagnosis, yet
somewhere, urgently, dead butterflies
confetti cotton fields
and flowers yawn open unpollinated

while here the train still clicks
metallic along familiar tracks;
following the same old route
between flowering trellises
as if all insects were not dying.

Doors flex open like elytra,
the engine's polished eye
unblinks. Passengers
rub against the pollen of this news,
carry it on their backs,
but, akin to bees, none can cry.

Home, on a street of honey-lit
suburban gardens, each fence regular as a wax cell,
a common carder bee has discarded herself,
left luggage on the hopeless pathway
of our front garden.

All around our shrubs are in full pompous colour,
a crowd of cheerleaders,
repeated in every garden.

Junk food. Hydrangeas are sterile,
nothing in them for a bee to eat.

You took me to the art house

Kettle's Yard, Cambridge

Our first lesson was about the lemon in Jim Ede's pewter dish,
how the waxed yellow orb forced a conversation
between paintings: a grey Wallis, a frowning Wood, a pollen
                                        dot in a Miro.

And then there was the way two broken shells were set
together on the mantelpiece, each shard reaching
round to pierce a balletic space in the other.

In the bathroom, empty shelves were as eloquent
as the masterpieces hung under the bay window,
the sailing boats and pebble spiral, best viewed from a rough
                                        wooden chair.

But as I passed from one room to another I became aware
– suddenly – of the light glancing on your tanned skin,
of the bones in your face, reaching round.

I sat in a wingbacked chair and regarded your long body,
framed in the gap made by a wall and a tall vase,
and I gazed at you, trying to decipher your gorgeous frown.

You stood at the table to read a letter from the archive
or bent to look more closely at an ancient flint
and I was grasshopper, intent, alert to your vibrations,

reading the language of your elbow's shape, the warm steadiness
of your breath, your hip's weight pressed into the table edge,
the crumb of lemon polenta cake resting on your lip.

Wind attempts a fox

1.

Wind, whisking in sycamore leaves,
restlessly stirs up.
Wants to make a fox out of autumn.

– Wind, pats narrow-footed through black leaf-litter earthsmell,
searching for that sunpatch place
where red fur folds up to sleep
russet and sharp with that stink of –

2.

Small breeze, noses
through October grass,
looking for conker eye-gleams,
pointed nose oak-apple,
yellow grass whiskers
hazelnut eye with a cowslip gleam
the longback haunchsprung form that can flow
waterlike over a wall
and disappear without –

3.

Wind, whirls up rusted maple leaves,
manages the snailcurl of a back,
red yawn shriek
the hot place cubs might slick from
the pant-yowl-
morningstar womb
dugs running with vixen's milk –

4.

Gusts, pant brown oak leaves into flanks.
Four dainty legs,

each not-quite-translucent chestnut hair tipped black,
teacup-rim jawline, porcelain,
ears pinned back listening,
almost blind mewing wet-bald closed-eye –

5.

Careful wind, brushes up beech leaves,
pine needles, hyphen eyes almost unsleeping,
a dream's rabbity twitch,
cold mist, like a morning's outbreath
from a fox's earth,
narrow foot scratching at the long strong
curve of a flea-blecked neck,
flank twitching, electrified itch,
jaws snap closed on a fly –

6.

Wind, breathes flames into sycamore,
yes, now dawn and stars join in,
oak branch, beechnut, hazel, ash leaf, holly thorn, pinecone,
spire of long grass, heliotrope, nova, moon –

7.

Ha! Fox!

Steps up from breathing,
unfolds delicate,
hand from a leather glove,
shakes nose to tail, gekkers,
breath puffballs ice,
yawns up, yowls up,
springs up, leaps up, earthbound – – – –

Gone.

Dying bee in a takeaway box (3)
Autobiography

I was nurse-queen or worker
I forget which for my small head
was uncapped inside the dark earth
long ago unsealed from propolis and
pollen store and my first taste
was ivy flowers oak roots and leaf litter
and that dark honey
that had been laid down over winter
in our deep mouse cellar –
such honey! a meat of dim wood-flowers
earth-stained and thick as blood –

and yes I was once a carder bee
serving a queen who was my mother
who named me and so only she knew how to call me
but I can hardly remember her
she has already been taken
you do not know my name
and there is nobody now
left to speak it.

The honey jar

I tore myself wide, just to make room for the honey jar.
I was all abdomen, barrel-round, a hive,
striped gaudy with stretch marks.

I was reconstructed as a mother made of wax. I left my old body
behind. Exoskeleton. The struts of the hive were
my ribs defending the colony. I could have swarmed

sent myself sonic screaming like a missile to the welcoming
void of a new trunk,
to safety. But I stayed, flower drunk.

My womb was a jewelled cellar, verdigris, amber.
I was bursting with it.
Gorged on honey, a fat, drowning sweetness.

Nothing of note had changed but the din of hearts.
I was heavy as a bulb. Luminous.

And then one midnight, I turned on my hip
and felt the jar crack.
I woke to honey down my thighs, drenching the bed,

everything running sticky and black. And there in the mess,
the queen,
beautiful as a daughter and softly drowned.

Rising through stars

6am lavender flower rising through stars notices a fox
nodding as it passes recognising the earth
willing itself up from soil

10am lavender beeflower tickled by the haired feet
of a red-tail bumble supping sugar water from the little
sucking mouths of buds gratifying itcher

11.30am lavender swaying in the kissing breeze
little alarmed spear
waves and swings in the pursed wind spilling grains

2pm spikeflower opening a bud unlatching petal lips
pushing from within forcing another purple flower
one more little mouth open coaxing nectar come on open

8pm little purple lavender poor thing
been too long unrained on
taproot drilling earth seeking cloud scat thirsting yellowed out

midnight black lavender in satin light breathing out spice
bruise smitten ant saunters glittering up the stem
pausing at the leaf joints to drink

6am lavender rising through stars
colled by the warm clouds fleeting across the moon
letting dust drift willing itself up from soil notices a fox

River Aire

you take me to where the river begins at Malham
rooted like a tongue
gurning from the depths of an old rock mouth
this is where you spring from

look down the valley's cleave
and there's the quicksilver pulled taut as a steel rope
hauled by an unseen sea
think of a giant's hands
heaving at the frayed end you say
              pulling at the river's fastenings

but it would rather move rock than give way
drag the cliff jawbone
like a snail setting out with the weight of a colossal wet shell
your eyes could be the river

we're married now flowing
and you wonder could water budge these cliffs?
they are scarred with grykes and clints
bothered   always this mithering
this scissoring of water
chopping at rock

your long bones and your lovely jaw
everywhere the water rebalances itself down levels
gipping as it chokes
against pebbles   coughing
on watercress
panicking under the flagstone cattle-bridge
mumbling to itself
some long unremembered song
stolen from an older river's throat

I understand you now
they call it the river Aire you say
this tongue in the rocks   flesh of water
limb reaching out of the mountain's joint

holding my hand with your limestone breath
your shoulder your cheekbone your thigh your blood
this husband place you've brought me
heartland where stone can be water can be air

The Mermaid

I.
The wind smacks its chops;
there's blood in the air.
I am called to the sea again.
The black claw beach is a litany of mussels,
each step a foot placed on uncertainty.
I perch in the twisted elbow of a drifted tree.
Where are you? I feel your wet eyes.

II.
There's a sinew in me now. They call it age.
But long ago I caught a mermaid,
untangled from a washed-up net.
Not a selkie nor a seal-sized girl,
but doll-like, pewter scaled, tiny as a chicken
bone. She clicked and curled
in my palm, spiked with seaweed fronds
and urchin spines; her tail delicate, lunate,
a slipping thing netted in my hand,
tense little mackerel girl.
At first her porcelain face seemed pained.
She made a birdlike scream. Then, calm,
her cheeks waxy, translucent as wet paper.
Coolly, she met my eye, batted
her tail like a coy eyelash.
Her arms fell to her sides,
showing her wrists to the stars.

III.
At home I made her a bed of cockles, whelks,
pebbles, in a tank topped up with brine.
I ignored the scratching in my stomach, a fool
distracted by my delight.

IV.
I slept that night as the dead sleep,
without dreams.
In the morning the pool was empty.
The mermaid had gone.
I felt a fingernail drag
down my belly, an eyelash flutter in the depths.
Something stirred inside.

V.
What I had done. The mermaid had taken me. I felt her hands
pressing to escape my skin.
Her heartbeat inside mine was the wave engine,
the sea's shrill.
My belly began to swell. I felt full of sweetness.
My veins showed bright on white skin. I grew cold.
I drank and drank.
Something shifted, stones in the grip of a riptide.
Her spines and thorns
marked me. I began to feel
a desperation of escape.

The sea went on singing its broken shellsong
and there was blood in the air, the salt wet tang of it.

VI
I gave birth to her on the sand.
When it was done, she cried,
red in her hair and on her hands.
She squirmed to get away from my heat
twisting towards the incoming tide.
I reached out for her, calling,
but she unfurled her butterfly tail,
her white back moonwards,
and slipped herself into a wave.
She didn't look back. Only swam
with a strong flick and dip to the ever-changing sea.

VII.
So long ago but still I search.
Each breaking wave might hold you, so I watch.
My scars are silver on this old skin,
Blue cools my blood.
I have lived too long,
my sad bones as ancient as the granite in my hand.
Each wave comes higher and a little higher.
I close my eyes.
I need only wait for high tide.

Airlings

Somebody has wrung them out
two rabbits, two dead rabbits
old flannels un-eyed and soft in their skins
as if the rain had hooked them from the air
twisted their lives out
wrung them out
two old flannels, loose knots
flung on a heap

flung
on a temple of old bracken
and dry grass, moving,
shushing, *shush*,

or are those fierce whispers
urging wake, wake,
remember?

remember how you ran
into the air,
you could hardly keep your feet,
barely pricked the soft pasture
as you leapt, always trying to free yourself,
flinging yourself skyward
your face turned towards light

but dragging the needle's thread
        the heavy gold thread of yourself
you buttoned your soft weight into the rising of the hill,
paused to press down the ploughed soil with your feet,
small brown pin.

I see now, you were the earth's beat,
her quick blood,
submitting to the arteries of the burrow
only for your dreams of the wind

among warm bodies strung, beads along the vessels,
rows of ears and feet,
each body a stitch in the seam,
     you hemmed the earth and the sky.

Shush now, shush, old flannels, wrung out on a heap,
your legs stretched long on the old dry grass,
listen how the wind sings,
her longing fingers in your fur as she whispers –
     come little airlings
     unbutton yourselves
     kick the light with your feet
     the earth can hold herself awhile.

Ninety-eight earth days

One day on Venus equates to 243 days on Earth

Child, you did not live a Venus day.
Forged in the spark of a boiling dawn
you were blind in her thick air. Slow

the sun scraped across the sky
and acid blasted your small breath, your mouth,
pinning you into her soft red hills, a moth

hunkering down, unable to fly.
Meanwhile we whizzed in dizzy time
across the great black clock face, the earth a second

hand dancing, looping through a day, another day,
and another, a jolly tachycardia,
carefree across the span of the galaxy, the lonely

black fall of space. You never cried
into the CO_2 of Venus' breast, but in the afternoon,
you found you had the energy to fail.

By then we'd spun around ninety-eight times on black ice,
dancing, dizzy, always looking for the sun, while you,
small as a lychee, lived your half day, dazzled, and died.

Dying bee in a takeaway box (4)
Out of time

The earth hears her small note.

Carder bee sings to herself
drags the empty basket of herself –

a honey memory
stirs –

tiny crotchet of hope

and yet stops. She is out of time.

Her crochet-hook feet
are feeble on the drumskin of the path.
A rest. She cannot find her beat.

But the earth hears everything.
Her heart's quiet fibrillations.
My children's footbeats as they run to fetch a spoon.
The rustle of processed sucrose tipping out.
The violin-string of her small wings, reverberating.

Lambs

every day we played in the field
until the sky cooled   the hot brick of August
weighing on our tent
my little sister a pale staggerer with a brown face
dwarfed by a patch of foxgloves
sunburnt spears rising through bees

we liked to send the sheep helter-skelter mad
I could *baaaa* like an old ewe
the lambs looked over, amazed

we harvested their fluff
from barbed wire
the lanolin smell crackling in our fingers

such a flock of triangle
heads always with a mouth of grass
on their delicate knees like pilgrims
praying greenery

at night
we safe in our sleeping bags
they in their wool

day after sheep day
we could taste them smell them hear them
breathed them in until we smelt of sheep
until we two stood among the tufted stars
in the constellation of their white flock

one night
a storm slunk through a sky-crack
like a collie's howl
turned the field to a wild green sea
untethered the old caravan
and sent it drifting, a crewless boat

the ewes burrowed down
as if the soil could harbour them
but in the morning
we found a dozen faces
        lambs and lamb-mothers stuck
        with their grass breath sweetening
        the dark place between the wheels

        we were lambs looking at lambs
hoping that the wind might trouble again
to lift the shipwreck from their backs
and set them back on their feet

paid a becso
I whispered to my sister a bleat of hope
that there was time to save
their black mouths from drowning
paid a becso again to the watchful faces in the dark
the caravan intent on pressing its weight down

soon Dad   breathing heavy
lifted enough
for the sheep to stagger up, out,
being careful to put his body between us
and the two slack lambs
left behind

The world begins & ends a billion, billion times

Bees see flowers with two compound eyes and three simple.
Flowers display bullseyes only visible under ultraviolet light.
The human ocular nerve is a taut string with cups at each end.
We see the world imperfectly through metaphors.

Poet. The world began on a sunny May day in 1977.
I view the world through a gap, a single glassy mosaic tile.
I see a glossy jackdaw through the glass tile, a baby's foot.
Through the glass tile I see daffodils bloom in snow.

Bee. The world began in a brown wax bowl in April last year.
I look at the world as a tracery of flowers and their goodness.
I see jealous lawns and nasturtiums cut down to size.
Through the glass tile I see ringed targets and forget-me-nots.

Oak. The world began four centuries ago in the shadow of a hazel tree.
I look through a glass tile at the jackdaws' nest
tickling at my wrist. Rickety corsage.
I look down at the hazel's crown, drowned in my shadow.

New queen. The world began this morning in the specific eye of a bungalow.
I look through the glass tile and see water flowing backwards.
I have made so much honey it drips down the living room walls.
My larvae swell. The river fattens up the hill.

Rain. The world began in a stump of rainbow not quite lifting out of my eye.
I saw a hawk drop through a glass tile as if on a cut string.
I flung myself onto the field.
I drenched and my throat fell open, and the world ended.

Dead king. The world began in Rome and my name is Julius Caesar.
I see through my glass tile, colourful grand mosaics.
Do you see now, the whole world is a glass picture made of a billion, billion tesserae?
One for each. For me the world has been, and been, and gone.

Storm Katrina. The world began in a carder bee's nest, April,
in combed chambers of sweet dry grass, round and perfect as hurricanes.
Mama, I'm tired and I want to lay down. Mama, I'm hungry.
The end of the world has already happened.

there was a time they were knotted to the riverbank

nested still as leverets in long grass
tickling in cow parsley and herb robert
to watch those kingfishers blink
binary   into existence, and out
there! the copper-blue quicker than her tongue
see how she pulls a fish from the river? (dad whispered)
then a gas flash and pluck up another jewelled minnow
        she? (shirley speaking, child's voice)
        so why not queenfisher?
and once   yesterday   a hundred years ago
        her father laughed

and her head was a wide river
minnowful, silver-scaled
she had more thoughts than there were salmon in the sea
she was a stream flashing with fat fish
        only   now she can't seem to hook them
            they say she can't remember

oh, there's the water now stay away from the mill pool
her father said   once yesterday   KEEP OUT!

or was it sister? *don't go out by yourself, shirley*

but, she knows her own mind and she is here,
trespassing on a cuckoo's summer, breathing the river's breath
what a summer she's inhaling
– who could forget those kingfishers?
fleeting flames striking on and off
reflecting   shining full of ken, full of riverknowing
like wisps sparking over water, and they, still as leverets

the tickle of long grass on her naked feet
where are they now?
but there are only empty sockets in the riverbank

where once they nested
don't go out they said
her hands are pale as a grayling's belly tickling under the surface

dad always knew what to do
would have taken her hand or stopped the river clutching at her
nightdress so
what a nuisance to be pulled out of herself like this   but
of course she knows

      the queenfisher will come, will reach down her flashing
beak
and take hold of her fingers
      she needs only look up through water and wait
      for the queen will lift her like a jewel to lie just there
      on the green bank with her father   and
      the brilliant wings will thrill again,
            to sound the echo of her heart's whir

Window

If I tell you this I will have to tell you
about the predetermined
cells of the body,
            the liquid accidental
collision of the smallest cell
and the largest

there in the caravan of my body, your future was foretold
the gold flecks in your eyes
balled-up with birdsong
blastocyst, cluster of yourself
lily exploding outward from the stem

inside the scarf of my belly you were not-yet-made
raw fibres
anything was possible
chromosomes knitted and purled:
you a finger, you an eyelash
you a kneebone, you a heart

you could have been whatever
a cry a tree a bird
but you were yourself brambling upwards, thorns clutching
and fruiting and you were sweet as a blackberry
spinal column arching upwards into juice
sparks from a new brain –
always so much your own

I could have wished for a window
a portal through muscle and blood, to watch
you, acrobat, whispering to yourself
I was scanning my whole body for newness
wondering what else you were up to
bumping the furniture around
shoving against the walls

but I didn't need a porthole: my heart was made of glass
ready to
break in emergency
anytime I wanted I could take out its telescope
look at you through its eye
watch your fingers drumming a new heartbeat
on the inside of my skin.

Dying bee in a takeaway box (5)
Ironic syrup recipe (for bees)

One quarter-teaspoon of granulated sugar,
dissolve in hot water,
a few drops from the cold tap.
Serve cool.

Notes:
The carbon footprint of beet sugar is 0.6 grams per gram.
Sugar beets are not permitted to flower
else their roots turn fibrous and lose their sweet flavour.

Crowsong

I used to think a crow's black
best described as an absence
      a hole cut into the sky

but under the bright blue lid of morning
I listen to crows cackle
      grate their larynxes
      like old wooden rattle crackers
and the meaning of absence becomes clear

they call for one of their own
the one who was dawn-plucked
in a feathered kerfuffle
swept off triumphantly
by the smallest spring fox

and I find the reality of absence is not after all
a black shape against blue
but the sound of the other crows
singing her name in their broken throats

Dying bee in a takeaway box (6)
Medicine

Spoon of sugar, medicine for a bee.
But nothing tells how to manage a bee
who will not take her dose,

who only folds herself in,
intent,
so very intent on her folding-in-ness,
as a daisy latching slowly inwards at dusk
so closing-in that she cannot think to take her medicine.

Instead she is nursed by the candle of her own quietness,
tasting mercury, glancing down at the clock on her chest,
measuring her vast distance from the sweetest centre of summer,
perhaps remembering
the countless flowers she tended in their beds.

The sacred well speaks to Mererid

[after dawn, a well centre stage]   I listen for the fall of your feet.
I know your steps as well as my own gelled atoms,
lovely girl   you are like water on stone
with the singing bell of your pail in your white hand.

[enter a girl, who dips her pail three times into the water] Drink
from me, singing girl,
you suck like a seal pup.
Drink my lovely
for beneath my low belly
the tide washes in and out calm as a moonflood.
Nothing can hurt you while you dip your pail into my water.

[the girl tips the water into irrigation channels below the castle keep]
Drink and pour my sweet water on the land,
little girl singing like a bell,
nothing can hurt you.

[the girl weeps] Don't look up wishing at the herring gulls,
my lovely, do not be fooled.
Their white wings are not free –
even they are shackled.
They cannot help but return to the sea. They will come again,
tomorrow and all the days afterward.

[enter the girl; the well sings] Drink, lovely girl with the white
hands,
do not chafe your mind at the horizon.
Drink and pour your water on the land.
Stay my lovely and suck your years into the sky and let the green
fields flow from your singing pail.
Drink and never stop   you must not fly away
for I and the green fields would weep for you.

[the stage is empty. The well calls for the girl]
Lovely girl the morning is old and you do not come.
Your pattering feet are silent as a dry river.
Why do the gulls circle and cry out?
My waters rise like blisters.
I cannot hold them.
You must suck, singing girl like a bell,
swinging your empty pail.

[the well's voice begins to waver] The tide swells like a bell's round belly. I
cannot stop her hunger!
She is coming up over the lip of the low hundred
seeking you, licking her tongue on the stones –
Mererid!

[the well calls a warning over the sound of noisy waves]
Return or the sea will find you, lovely girl,
and all your green fields
your homesteads and horses
and all your people, your men and your women and your babies,
will be salted with her tears.

[The girl does not come. A deluge floods the stage.]

36

The Llanlleonfel church yew

you presided eight hundred winters
with your gnarled stick your knees pressed into soil
owls nestled on the altar of your tufted hair
old woman old bent woman
you no longer creak in your bones
and the Ancient Yew Group
mourns your bitter end

for when the woodsman came
to tidy up your skirts
to keep you from overshadowing the mourners
his cuts were too young for you too keen
the members of the Ancient Yew Group
found your green throat silenced
beneath his wasping saw
left loose-toothed among the gravestones
naked as an earthbone
your hair shorn
your trunk's tender skin weeping
and you   unlimbed

                  no more than heartwood
                  obscene wood stump

and so when I stood
        sipping my breath
with my hand flat on the hospital door
about to go in but listening

        listening in that small infinite pause

                to my womb's gate banging in the wind and
                other people's babies crying thinly in their milk
                with my pale-moon sister newly mothered
                and my tiny niece just there
                in the room beyond my hand

I understood the simple grief
of what it meant
to be reduced to a twist of stump

with only the dry muscle of my wooden heart
        protruding from the earth
        unroofed unloosed to the weather
and finding there no place for owls to sleep.

Wasps

They couldn't be further from lullabies
    pins-and-needles on the fly,
    wing-tangles,
    malicious sizzle on a sleeve.

    They fold around my fingertip
    tweezing with legs,
    jawing,
    a jazz cymbal buzz that will reverberate
    through my bones all afternoon.

They alarm the air
    closed circuit surveillance
    on every ice cream/ sausage/ cider.

    Black-goggled yellow jackets,
    drones, armaments,
    bullying out the smallest excuse to sting.

They are exocet
    sugared-up venom
    drunk on spilled juice and bruising for it.

    Occupying the quiet valleys of our heads,
    belligerent, generals and scouts,
    raiding beneath the auspices of an unseen queen.

They mesmerise, beads strung from wire,
    any moment we'll collide,
    and then the shriek in the ripest apple,
    a bitter pip, darting our little girl's lip

    and the sound that is
    a million miles from lullabies.

Dying bee in a takeaway box (7)
Wild colony collapse

Foulbrood, chalkbrood, stonebrood.
This war is fought on the wing
blown by sullen winds
or taken in on an almond-tasting tongue.
Our mating is an unwitting dogfight.

On the ground we face unicellular invasions,
bacterial, viral,
fungal bodies that eat
us out from the middle
till we flake like old paper.
Mites savour our taste,
leave us bloodless,
a hollow infantry.

Only the old queen outlives,
far behind the battle lines,
while foragers and mates
are felled alike.
Are felled, so the brood falls too.

A new frontier dawns,
the terror of cross-infection.
Honey is a nail-bomb.

Dying bee in a takeaway box (8)
Clock

This
bee
is
a
stopping
clock
on
the
path,
ticking
irregular
time.

Her wings are folded together:
a strung up
midnight,
hands at prayer.

Woodthinking

once you understand
    that trees are earthed on a tipped compass
            that air   you can know
  is the water where they dip their toes
        not through the breath   exhaled from wooden lungs

                a steady intention of intellect
but as a creature stirring in the earth beneath

    bound into a great root ball   electric impulses of soil

                        fibrous earth as a medium of thought

you can listen –
to ancient knowings
listen –
for the creak begins there
where the tree first uncurled from
its gleaming seed
and turned two ways
there
in the small songs of the saprising
an oak clockwork set
to the round-ringing ribboning of seasons
pushing up
numberless clinker-built ribs

                    that rise and clasp
                        and rise

                                        branchwires drill down
            but also from this dark fist of roots
                        the trees' nerves   the tympan   straining
vertebrate
        a long ear horned into the ground
            attending feverishly to the earth's mutter

    listen!
nonsense and   secrets   the world scrabbling and worming   lousing to itself

— why has nobody thought
    to change the words for   where a tree thinks?
                                        for there is no electric beat at the head
                                in the wind-rustle of the green leafcrown
    in the heartwood of the trunk   nor in the muscles of the leaning limbs

                woodthinking   is a brain in soil

            it is there   deep in those thrilling roots   where the whole wood
        gathers itself
to listen
        listen and marvel   at the shuffle of worms

43

Dying bee in a takeaway box (9)
Body

a Bee is not a Bee.
a Bee is only this:
a simple cell, emBryo,
a single golden hair
which eBBs and falls unheeded.

she is not more.
not a self of her own, but noBody.
as a Blood cell is not a self
only carries its heart's Burden
in good faith, But without intention. aBsolved

she is not more than the single viBration of a hive's heart
while the heart Beats elsewhere,
rumBling in the hive's riB.

the Body is colony
conglomeration of cells,
weather event, a swarm
aBsorBed, intent on its Business.
and the colony is also
endlessly self-making, carBon copying,
seeding and reseeding,
each Bee giving its small Body for this Body.

at season's end only a single seed is needed,
Banked up in the Brazier of the queen's Bronze forge,
the Body soon to Be reBorn.

Gaslight

Not long after you arrived
we lay swaddled together in bed
you and I, our bodies small
on the corner of the sheet like two buildings
marked on a map.

You were sucking on my milk
sanding against me with the love of your tongue
breaking the barrier of skin between us.
You couldn't have got closer,
your living system jacked into mine.

You sucked until I bled and my breasts
thickened, clotted, turned hard,
and your little sucking breaths
their over-and-over-again beat,
became the only sound I could hear

until I looked down and found that the walls
had fallen away. Above and all around
I saw the night sky in its terrifying glory
each cold, unreachable star,
flickering, as if the gaslight glow
powering each one
was altered by some process
far out of my understanding.

The pulse that passed between us was the
sound of the whole universe.
I was only alive to keep you alive.
An overheating boiler,
my life's manual already written,
unalterable. I saw the trick that had been played.
Joy, curiosity, work, study, being a good person.
None of these mattered at all. Only you,

breathing in, breathing out,
my life for yours.

And that is how it was, how it went on,
until someone came
into the room, and flicked on the lights.

You can play water

At Limeslade, the first stone dropped
into the rock pool makes a musical note.
Then a second. Deep bass pianos in the shadows,
the shallows offer high peals.
We find more stones, limestone, flint, quartz.

Like pearls, round pebbles glim from your small hands
and slip down, embraced by the water's surface.
The pool rings and chimes and tines.

You like the sounds of stones.
At your clacks, crabs flex back under the rocks –
the plack of stone on wet stone
startles shrimps into the sun.

We try to play a tune, rough pebbles and smooth,
dark and light like piano keys,
flying from our dry hands into the wet
trombone mouth as it flings notes back into air:
         plink, che-kunk, plip, chewp, blup

You give the water voice.
And, oh! It sings.

Dying bee in a takeaway box (10)
Queen

I know what it is to be a hive,
to have workers in and out of my belly
laying down their store.
I know the apiarist's gloved touch.
I have been Langstroth, waiting for nuclei.
Framed by empty chambers, defined by them,
by the want of honey.
Longing for that sweetness on my tongue.

They pulled enough drawers out of me,
breathing through masks,
the honeycomb dripping,
decorticated the layers, shoved back again.
And still, nothing buzzed.
How could you not feel it,
the physical gape of the hive refusing
to swell, winter on its way
and still nothing?

In the end, it had happened. I had been colonised,
my life slipped through the lens.
I bulged like a fallen question mark.
Inside, the queen lay down lines.
I felt the sparrow quickness of her wings in the dark.
Each small movement filling another fat cell.
The honey heaven of it,
the blossom of myself, the sureness.
How the new queen made us both
alive. Despite knowing the walls
were only made of wax.

Sonication

I am more than you.
I am a musical note.
My body makes the colour of a middle C.

Flowers clutch their pollen
tight as pearls but my thorax,
abdomen, hindlegs, forewings,
mandibles, antennae, tongue –
together transform, hum, and then I become
a trembling vibrating perfect note.
Sonicating.

My body is diva.
And when I hit my note they throw flowers,
drench their pearls down my back.

The swing

Six years on but still, sometimes,
the woman
pushing the swing, still there,
do you remember?

I wake and find you in the dawn,
from the mother-and-baby group,
in that playground –
both of us in the park:

your older daughter is
her legs flying up
as she leaves you and comes back,

straddled into the safety swing,
towards the sun
leaves you, and comes back

and I am
the wind insisting itself
the row of boats along the foreshore
ringing,
my own baby snug
and her small,
working,

with you,
into everything,
with their metalwork
crying out,
in the hull of her pram,
reliable, heart
winging in its chest

so that when I gull myself next to you
about motherhood –
miss
locked onto you,
as she reluctantly leaves you,
a series of
her swoop,
each time caught uncertainly
between soaring joy

– squawking too noisily
I almost
your daughter's eyes,
airborne tight,
and leaves you,
small griefs,
her snag of delight,
in that belly-drop moment
and parting.

I was too slow to notice   you were a cracked egg,
albumen   leaking out of you,
the way you forced yourself   to push the swing away,
willed your muscles to obey,   each push a wrench of the heart.

I presumed you had simply left your baby boy with your mother.

But of course,   there are your daughter's eyes,
fixed on you   as you slowly implode – you,
with your heart   strung up on a pendulum –
transfixed,   watching you
caught in that terrible   moment between:

oscillating, flying away,   hands outstretched
for the miraculous return.

Dying bee in a takeaway box (11)
Spark

Late in the season, a dusk of gasping.
Now the body must dissolve,
the colony set itself in store.

First: break into pieces.

This is how she endures, nameless dying bee,
as a small note, a telegram
kept lantern within
the torch carried by another,
buried in the deep till spring.

Somehow the smallest spark will survive
winter's savage kiss from inside
the pocket of its cheek.

In two hearts

Oh Mag
I long for you until
I can't seem to speak. Can't do
anything but croak and shuffle my old wings.
Nights and days swing by
and sometimes I lift my head
and find I am hoared over with frost,
as if I am dressed in white lace
for your return.
I wait for the creak of you, but you do not come.

February

Mag,
Have you heard their rhyme? The little girls
in the garden, sitting in red coats,
singing *one for sorrow, two for joy.*
The words tine through my bones.
Don't you see? I am the one,
folded in sadness;
this nest-dark place.
Oh when will you come back?

March

Dearest Mag,
I am sorry for the pity of my last lines.
Perhaps all I needed was
the gold coin of the sun to rise
and shine in my eye, a garnet, a gleam.
I've got my glimmer back now,
the same old girl you knew before.
The nest rings like a bell when I land.

I settle my feathers on wedding bands
like eggs of gold.
I know you will come back.
I will look for your wings making their wishbone shape.

April

Mag,
Still you do not come.
I am in two hearts,
one heart of white and another of black.
As if a black bird and a white bird
collided in air to make me.
How can you keep yourself from me?
Sometimes I feel I might die from
the coal despair of myself
a gone-out fire.
But my white heart flares
knowing you would never leave me.
Certain that you are fighting
darkness to get back to your poor
dove-heart, your only girl.
I wait for night to be over.
Say you will come, my love,
Bring me the moon on silver wings.

May

My lost Mag,
I wait.
Two birds nest nearby
Their love drums through the trees.
I smell it like lilies.
I sicken.
My black eyes close.
I try to watch for you over the sharp blade
of the sea. You are lost treasure.

I hoard all I have left,
memories and trinkets. I think I am cursed.
I presume you have flown
to a land of better things.
You are not coming and you will not come.
Those birds. The boy and girl. I see them.
They watch to see when I might leave.
They've got their eyes on our gold things
and I am trapped on the nest, guarding your heart.
I wonder, then, whether I am a fool.
You have gone to some other girl, some other pie
your heart rings for another dove-heart.
Perhaps you would not mind, love, if I spread my wings?

June

Mag,
I cannot abide the heat.
It consumes me so I can hardly breathe. There is no place
to escape the searing sun.
I hate that you have not returned.
Gold is an unforgiving pillow on my poor breast.
I cannot find comfort anywhere.
Why have you not come for me?
Mag, I know now that you are cruel.
I remember how often you hurt me.
I twist in secrets.
It comes to me now that I hate you, my love.
I hate you. I hate you. I hate you.

July

My darling
You must think me very foolish for my last words.
Of course I do not hate you
I only mourn you, thinking of each moment apart
as a piteous waste when we could have

tucked together like two pages of a letter.
I dream of you, love, of your wings opening wishlike
and your heart longing for mine as mine longs for yours.
I am so hungry. I must try to eat.

August

Oh Mag!
Thank you! Thank you! Thank you!
I have received your surprise!
I do not understand why you waited until I had left
– it was only for a moment –
but oh my love I forgive you!
Now at last
I know you are here
I found an astonishment in the nest
another gold ring, my love,
nothing but another gold ring!
Only you know the golden secrets of our two hearts
so I know it must have been you.
Oh Mag, I am so close to you. I can taste your sweet kisses!

September

My dear lost Mag,
What a misery I have been under.
It has taken me thirteen days to come to it
but I know my mistake. I am a fool, miscounting.
I have numbered them again and again
and my heart shatters to find my folly.
I count only two rings.
and yet I was so certain.
How can a solid gold circle
disappear as if it were a shadow?
Now the sun bids me farewell, too.
Yesterday I heard your voice calling my name
but woke to find my own throat hoarse.

October

You are gone. I know it now.
You will not return to me.
In my dreams I remember
looking down the garden
and seeing a dying bird.
His filmy eyes blinked, his crooked wings
tried to lever the air
but he was stuck to the earth.
Around him I counted six magpies watching, guarding.
They called and called as if to wake him,
and all the wood stopped still
to listen for his answer. But he could not lift his head.
He was their brother, the seventh.
All afternoon they waited, guarding the spark in his eye.
When his heart stilled
they rose into the air together,
calling him home.

November

Mag,
Do you think that dream was about me?
Am I dying, my love?
Or was it nothing but a story?
Perhaps I should not have told you.
Some things should not be spoken.
If I close my eyes or look into the moon,
will you come for me at last?

December

My love,
I dream you are my brother.
It is snowing
silent and white and wonderful

as though moonflakes were coming down
pieces of sorrow and joy.
This is my heart.
I know where you are now, darling Mag,
and I am coming to find you my love.
I have plucked out my black feathers.
I am coming to find you with white wings.

The Green Pages

A found directory of the apocalypse

Boat hire

Voyages of Discovery. The owl and the pussycat
painted on a smashed green hull. Bottlenose dolphins rear up
over broken boat backs, smiling. There is no engine noise,
anywhere. Wildlife safaris. A billion puffins roost
unfilmed on the grassy clifftops, feeding fresh herring to their young.

Conservatories

The Everest van is parked outside No 26. Installing
quality. Adding extra living space.
The house is leafed out, possessed, congested with green.
The walls bulge. Red squirrels flow from sill to sill. Oak trees
elbow up through PVC frames. Jackdaws tag their branches.

Electricals

Evans & Son. In a cable stack, an adder has coiled her
might around her eggs, twitching to see a mouse eat what's left
of an ancient packet of ginger biscuits. Mr Evans' favourites.
All types of machine fixed. Free visual
inspections. Over in the workshop he is no more than a
grin in a pile of bleached bones.

Financial advisers

30 million hedgehogs are snouting in the black now,
multiplying. They eat the woodlice that feast on wet computer
paper at Wealth Management Ltd. Lifetime
Mortgages. Pamela Thomas's unpaid bills. Red ink tastes
the same.

Firewood

Valley Timber. A skyful of fluffed-up goldfinches needles
for flies in the snowberries behind loose loads & netted logs.
Keep warm this winter. The heating pipes in the

warehouse have long since split and drenched everything. A stag beetle – unseen in these parts for a century – lumbers over a box file arched with damp.

Funeral directors
Arthur Cambrey's family-run business. `Large parking area. Private Rooms. Chapel of Rest.` Nothing grows. No living thing comes. Foxes are too busy making out in the jacket hedgerows of the high street.

Tree work
Water pours down the hill. The reservoir is breached. Translucent letters float by. `Arboretum Ltd.` John's safety gauntlet barely afloat. The yard, underwater now, flicks cleverly with pike, chub, bream. The river rises. On a log lifted by water, a thousand speckled wood butterflies lay their eggs.

Yacht charterers
The reservoir, the sea, the wood. *Turn to: Boat hire.*

Silverfish live on my daughters' crumbs

Snap on the light and silver shivers towards dark –
      sardine shine at the room's skirts
      where slick land prawns shoal
      to lap sugar that falls from your lips.

Unseen, they half-see through compound eyes
      set in a half-moon fingernail scale
      of undulating body. The whisk and turn
      at the eyelash edge of a girl's sight.

Nymphs! The silverfish watch you age,
      their Palaeozoic hearts tick unchanged
      in the armour of metal chests.
      They gleam into wrinkles before you can touch them.

Your hair tickles the leather
      suite, clings down. They can only marvel
      at how it multiplies, cell by cell, as you sleep –
      how you never stay the same.

Dying bee in a takeaway box (12)
Wind

You were born in a furnace, on the coal of a maternity bed
delivered from the anvil of my bones.
Hospital boilers worked overtime.
Nurses and doctors seemed oblivious to the heatwave outside,
cars shimmering like liquid.
We gleamed. You were alloy, forged,
made in a smithy from the panting bellows of my chest.

When I peeped past curtains
the sea was a mirage, a blue hallucination.
Daughter, I was tired. Soft, pliable, with no idea how to love
you, no idea how to make myself sturdy enough for the task.
Worn out by the shock to my heart of seeing your perfection.
Everything waited for me to come round, even the air.
The whole building was stiff with waiting.

I know what you're wondering.
Where was the wind in all of this?
Everybody needs air. Even fire.
But someone had painted the hospital windows shut.
I started drowning in that room, trying
not to break you, your brittle cry, trying
to stop it from falling like glass on the hard floor,
from shattering into locked doors.

But wait, did I ever tell you about the bee? The bee *is* breath,
a chamber of restless air, a lung transposed into breeze.

The bee doesn't breathe.
She allows the air to pass through her.

Remember that. She *allows* air.

Your father saved us. He could see the bee
I had become, hollow, spiracled, a dead seed head,
how I could only breathe
by means of the breeze passing through.
He carried us both away to the woods by the seashore.

And now I have told you everything you need to know.
Look at her there, on the path, as she leaves herself.
This carder bee as tired as a mother. So many sleepless nights, wet beds.
The wind shoving at her, nagging. Live, live.
She is dying. She has already died.
She no longer allows the bother of air.
I feel her departure inside myself.

A dead bee in the Lego

There's a dead bee in the Lego,
his soft thorax an understated gleam
amid the polychromatic blocks
that jag the laminate floor.

It's uncomfortable to imagine
the last moments of the bee.
Perhaps these jubilant colours
reminded him of a summer meadow.

What a disappointment
to flick his tongue in hopes
of honeysuckle, and find only
acrylonitrile butadiene styrene.

The Circle

Bodø, Norway, 2018

they are waiting

for the end of the pause
that keeps their snow a ghost
a wet wool taste furring the wind
that keeps groundmelts like clear eyes
reflecting herring-gulls and strange halflight
instead of hard marbling puddles
to cataracts
      they wait

for summer to finish her long outbreath
into their mouths
boats groaning at ropes
fish straining in water
stirring the surface from beneath
as if the long-drowned reach up
to feel for the usual ice lid
      they are waiting

for ships moored at the end of each road
to pull and shatter their white chains
or to find the mountain
dressed in a white coat too tight for her hips
for the dark of dreams
to enfold their heads
as if the midnight sun had never risen
was no more than a fancy

for the unthawing
for the comfort of the candlelit lock-in
for the clasping creaking
clench the herring-cold reek

that means winter has returned to the Arctic
     they are waiting

but it is late and sunsets are still tender on the water
birch trees gleam full-leaved
far south cherry blossom blooms for the second time in Japan
and here daylight clings like seals' milk –

    what if one day winter might forget them altogether?

each year a little later
a little less
in icelessness
     they wait

Dying bee in a takeaway box (13)
Below the fold

I lay out the little carder bee
on newspaper from the train.
A female. Her pollen baskets full.

Catastrophic insect population collapse.
Roughly four hundred words.
Every one must be made to count.

She is tracing-paper light
miraculous across the headline
laid flat in an old noodle box.

Below the fold
the newspaper buzzes
its alarm. Other news is taking up space.

Bread and butter

I'm wondering what love is
standing at the kitchen counter
crumbling ear-soft white bread into an enamel bowl
butterflies   full of wings with my bones tired
as you laugh with your father in another room

Is this love?
fetching you home after the day's electric forest-floor scrabblings
standing at the kitchen counter
emptying incessant woodlice from my brain
watching as they trundle across the tiles
crumbling too-soft bread ear-soft
until my fingers ache
patient, while millipedes scrabble from my ears, scrawl over the cutting board
chopping thin slivers of chicken
as you laugh with your father in another room

is it love to melt butter in a pan?
salting breadcrumbs, pressing in pink strips of ear-soft chicken
while moths stuff paper wings in my nose and mouth   crumbling
the yeast smell rising – surely love's wholesome scent –
as you laugh with your father in another room

Is it love to lay the finger-thin shreds in the frying pan?
standing at the kitchen counter
fizzing with earwigs
the sigh and sizzle as bread and hot butter meet
the rosy chicken flesh milking up
as you laugh with your father in another room

Is it love to hand you the dish?
each golden morsel gleaming
standing at the kitchen counter
earthworms churning in the leaf litter of my skull
as you laugh with your father

handing over the plate
skittering scrabbling stuffed
knowing you won't even eat it anyway.

School run

You gave me your camellia flower, bright as a shepherd's warning.
It filled your outstretched palms, its gorgeous mouth open.
You put it on my flat palm and told me, be careful mamma.
I left you at the school gates and ran home, balancing.
The flower funnelled rainwater onto my hand – clear, gluey.
I passed the camellia bush, bleeding its flowers on the pavement.
Yesterday it had been a yellow snail shell, curled foetal.
As a girl, I walked this way from school, past gardens, to my grandparents' house.
Pavements cannot love, but they can catch your falling feet.
Camellias are symbolic of the divine, of children, of longevity.
Every day you take such a long time to walk up the hill into the winter sun.
This road is rooted in us; you shrub your way up into girlhood.
Every worm, every flower, a pause. My hands are wet – running, honeyed.

The winter-king

little-word bird little wren
feathered lung only built for singing
purifying freezing air through
a feather ball chitter chatter piper
little wren little brownleaf keeneye
built for singing
round like a minim
little wren pink wire feet
gripping winter's branches
holding on to cold little bird
only built to pipe built to whistle
keeneye watching snow fall
crowning the holly little thornbeak
feathered bauble hanging on the pine
only built to sing
turning cold air into arias
too quick for the ice to catch
little keeneye raised eyebrow
jingling the dead leaf bells
surely too small to be—
but they say you're the winter-king
only you can sing us into light

Bee in a January Pilates Class

The queen overwinters with last year's sperm parcelled
in her abdomen's bronze urn, the coming summer's
colony in store. She will decide male/female, holds
the power over what sort of eggs to lay, what number.
She sleeps now, above us, in the casing of a fluorescent bulb,
a clear buzzing coffin that lights our larval limbs, C-curled
or Z-sat, scissoring, full-body stretching, abdomen, tibia,
metatarsus, tarsus. Tucking in honey stomachs overfilled
in December, we spine-roll down, breathing.
                                        Bumble bees do not breathe.
Air passes through spiracles to mingle with the blood
which pools around the organs, a heart that seethes
the full body's stretch, a humming tube unsettling a flood.
Our false sunshine has tricked her awake, and now she clambers
up, out; we, prone, as she drones, vibrates, clamours.

Silk buttons

Late August in the woods and the gall wasps
have sewn their buttons to the oak.
We don't know about them yet –
underside stitchers, hiding their trove on the pale
backs of leaves. You found their sign, the open-mouth
graffiti studding mother oak's leaves,
like something from your playlist, *Oh, Oh, Oh*.

Look, Mum! A Tudor tapestry of gold circlets
riveted by the spindles of a thousand
fingernail queens. Such secrets planted in the oak's green realm.

This is our last summer with you like this.
You are eleven, a bud unfurling. *Is magic real?* you ask.
Only if you believe.
You have your doubts. But we keep our eyes open
for *tylwyth teg* along the canal. You spin ahead on the path
in red waterproofs with arms wide, hair flying.

Last year we stood on these banks and heard
a cuckoo call. Searched for kingfishers, but never saw one.
Your gran said she spotted otters here last month,
their backs shaping the water as if the surface had come alive.
We won't see one today. A storm's coming.
The canal jitters in anxious waves.

I am afraid to break the spell
of childhood in you. Your waterlily eyes,
hair flying up like swallows, arms out
in spindle points. Patchwork daughter.
I made you out of stories. You are Red
Riding Hood, Beth climbing the Faraway Tree,
Arachne weaving her silken threads.
Blodeuwedd, the girl made of flowers, an owl
sparking up behind your eyes.

You pull your phone from your pocket, take a photo
of the galled leaves. In that lit square a new generation waits.
We have been blind to their buzz,
deaf to their dancing: miniature queens,
stitching their gold in the seasons.

Soon we've Googled them.
We have discovered the magic of their silk buttons,
the larvae inside, how these sleeping beauties, all female,
carrying spells, the incantations of their future queendoms,
are fastened in tight for winter, ready to fall with the leaves.
How they will emerge from next year's shoots,
as soon as summer returns,
splendid and shining in their bright new skins.

Stories

This moon dark is owl-less, and the stars are like
small white hands pressed against
the night's belly. Sometimes I look
up, knock the thin bones of my skull on the window pane,
a trapped bee. Behind me in the room, you.
Two girls and their father.
You know my heart's song as though
you have lived another life inside it.
I can score from memory the busy comings and goings of yours.
Stories buzz from the honey circle
of your lamp's light, as if nothing
had ever stung us at all, and nobody knew anything about the pain of a sting.

Girls, if you want to hear them, I know a few stories about bees.

For example. In Welsh, they call the hive, *cwch gwenyn,*
a bees' boat.
I think of it as a lifeboat. It sails on, out
over the warming waves. The four of us are tucked
safe as love letters in the hull of the hive's curved ribs.

For example. Bees make music. A perfect Middle C.
They can sonicate their whole bodies into a musical note.
They are divas, sopranos, titillating flowers until
a shower of pollen pours down their backs.

For example. In ancient Egypt, bees were the tears
cried by the sun god Ra.
They carried messages to earth from the heavens
and accompanied the dead to the afterlife.
I like to imagine them,
tending each star as though it is a flower.

Now, tell me what you have learned.
Bees carry messages. Yes. They cross storms, seas,

black rivers, they cross whole winters. Good. Bees are a living love song.
Bees make skies bloom, attend the dead,
carry a seedbank of the living.

Now for a new story. We put all of our hope in one bee.
She is a vessel, an amber honey jar. Think of her,
deep in the earth, waiting in the dark for her time,
the pulsing spark on an ultrasound scan.
Now understand that there are more of her. One bee,
and one bee, and one bee. Each one a seed holding seeds.

The story does not end. It sonicates.

Notes

The lines from 'The Bee Mother' by Pascale Petit are taken from her collection *The Treekeeper's Tale* (Seren, 2008).

The quote from *Why Rebel* (Penguin, 2021) by Jay Griffiths also appeared in her defence statement at court, when she was tried under the Public Order Act for the occupation of Oxford Circus in April 2019 as part of Extinction Rebellion protests. Her full statement can also be found online and is well worth reading.

The Dunns

This poem is written as a response to 'Adlestrop' by Edward Thomas, first published in the *New Statesman* in April 1917.

Wind attempts a fox

gekker – to make the chattering, stuttering sound particular to foxes

River Aire

grykes – fissures that separate clints in a limestone pavement
clints – blocks forming part of a natural limestone pavement
mithering – Yorkshire dialect for moaning
gipping – Yorkshire dialect for retching

Lambs

paid a becso – Welsh for don't fret

The sacred well speaks to Mererid is based on the Welsh myth of Cantre'r Gwaelod in which an area of low-lying land off the coast of modern-day Cardiganshire was flooded. In more recent versions of the myth, a drunk man by the name of Seithennen is blamed for drinking too much beer at a feast and falling asleep, neglecting his duty to close the sluice gates that protected the land and villages from the tide, resulting in the land being flooded and the villagers drowned. But older versions of the story blame the young maiden Mererid for the disaster. It was her role to appease the water goddess by taking

76

water from the sacred well every day and pouring it into channels that kept the land watered and fertile. Travellers came from around the world to see the legendary green lands of Cantre'r Gwaelod, but their stories of far-flung places tempted Mererid to leave her duties, which angered the goddess and resulted in the flood.

Silk buttons

tylwyth teg – Welsh for fairies

Acknowledgments

Several poems from this collection were first published in journals including *Poetry Wales, Poetry Ireland, Marble, New Welsh Reader, Magma, The Cardiff Review, The Bay Magazine, Envoi* and *The Rialto*.

Recordings of a selection of these poems being read by the author are available at iambapoet.com.

'The winter-king' won the Rialto Nature and Place Poetry Competition and 'Airlings' won the Welsh International Poetry Competition. 'The swing' was shortlisted for the Winchester Poetry Prize, 'Bread and butter' longlisted for the Mslexia Women's Poetry Competition, and 'The sacred well speaks to Mererid' shortlisted for the PenFRO prize. 'School run' was published in the Poetry Business anthology, *The Result is What You See Today*.

I would like to say a special thank you to my family for their love, support and encouragement, and for hopefully not minding too much that I write poems about them: my husband Phil and our daughters, Gwennan and Mabli; my wonderful parents and cheerleaders, Joy and Meirion; and my sister Jo and her family – Owen, Ffion, Iestyn and Lwsi.

I must also mention my dear friends and fellow poets: Jean James, Lesley Williams, Maggie Blewitt and the late and much-missed Glenda Davies. We met at a poetry class and have become lifelong friends. Equally, thanks go to the Salty Poets – Emily Vanderploeg, Rhys Owain Williams, Alan Kellerman, Natalie Ann Holborow, Mari Ellis Dunning and Adam Sillman, who have been enormously welcoming, generous and funny.

My gratitude to Susie Wildsmith for her expert editing of this volume, as well as to the team at Parthian. Thank you for making my book a reality.

And finally, in memory of our two lost babies, who were too briefly treasured, and never forgotten.

I hope you will take a moment now to go outside with your eyes and heart open, and listen to the bees.

PARTHIAN *Poetry*

How to Carry Fire
Christina Thatcher
ISBN 978-1-912681-48-8
£9 | Paperback
'A dazzling array of poems both remarkable in
their ingenuity, and raw, unforgettable honesty.'
– Helen Calcutt

Sliced Tongue and
Pearl Cufflinks
Kittie Belltree
ISBN 978-1-912681-14-3
£9 | Paperback
'By turns witty and sophisticated, her writing shivers
with a suggestion of unease that is compelling.'
– Samantha Wynne-Rhydderch

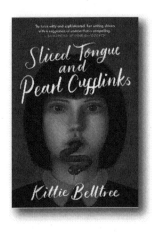

Hey Bert
Roberto Pastore
ISBN 978-1-912109-34-0
£9 | Paperback
'Bert's writing, quite simply, makes me happy.
Jealous but happy.'
– Crystal Jeans

PARTHIAN *Poetry*

Windfalls
Susie Wild
ISBN 978-1-912681-75-4
£9 | Paperback

'Powerful, beautifully crafted poems…
there's nothing like poetry to cut down the spaces
between us, to leap across gaps,
make a friend of a stranger.'
– Jonathan Edwards

Small
Natalie Ann Holborow
ISBN 978-1-912681-76-1
£9 | Paperback

'Shoot for the moon? Holborow has landed, roamed its face,
dipped into the craters, and gathered an armful of stars
while up there.'
– Wales Arts Review

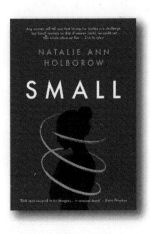

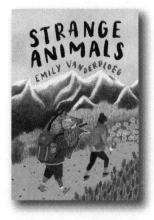

Strange Animals
Emily Vanderploeg
ISBN 978-1-913640-70-5
£9 | Paperback

'Emily Vanderploeg's clear-eyed lyric poetry explores the
questions of where we belong, who we have become, and who
or what undertakes that journey alongside us.'
– Carolyn Smart

PARTHIAN *Poetry & Prose*

Gorwelion: Shared Horizons
Edited By Robert Minhinnick
ISBN 78-1-913640-55-2
£9 | Paperback

'This project aims to imagine what life in Wales could look like in the future as seen through the lens of the cultural dimension of well-being.'
– Sophie Howe, Future Generations Commissioner for Wales

Gorwelion – Shared Horizons is a climate change anthology of poetry and prose edited by prize-winning writer and environmental activist Robert Minhinnick featuring Welsh, Scottish, Indian and English writers. Produced in collaboration with Sustainable Wales/Cymru Gynaliadwy.

Riverwise:
Meditations on Afon Teifi
Jack Smylie Wild
ISBN 978-1913640-39-2
£9 | Paperback

'(A) fine, absorbing and wonderfully attentive book' **– Nation.Cymru**

Riverwise is a book of wanderings and wonderings, witnessings and enchantments, rememberings and endings. Weaving memoir, poetry and keen observation into its meandering course, it shifts across time and space to reflect the beauty of hidden, fluvial places, and to meditate on the strangeness of being human. A clarion call to learn to love and protect the natural world and its waterways.

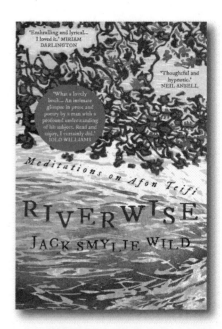

'Enthralling and lyrical...
I loved it.' MIRIAM
DARLINGTON

'Thoughtful and hypnotic.'
NEIL ANSELL

'What a lovely book... An intimate glimpse in prose and poetry by a man with a profound understanding of his subject. Read and enjoy, I certainly did.'
IOLO WILLIAMS